MINI MAKERS

Mini HOLIDAY CRAFTS
TO CELEBRATE in STYLE

by Rebecca Felix and
Ruthie Van Oosbree

CAPSTONE PRESS
a capstone imprint

Dabble Lab is published by Capstone Press, an imprint of Capstone.
1710 Roe Crest Drive, North Mankato, Minnesota 56003
capstonepub.com

Copyright © 2024 by Capstone. All rights reserved. No part of this publication may be reproduced in whole or in part, or stored in a retrieval system, or transmitted in any form or by any means, electronic, mechanical, photocopying, recording, or otherwise, without written permission of the publisher.

Library of Congress Cataloging-in-Publication Data
Names: Felix, Rebecca, 1984- author. | Van Oosbree, Ruthie, author.
Title: Mini holiday crafts to celebrate in style / by Rebecca Felix and Ruthie Van Oosbree.
Description: North Mankato, Minnesota : Capstone Press, a Capstone imprint, [2024] | Series: Mini makers | Includes bibliographical references. | Audience: Ages 8 to 11 | Audience: Grades 4-6 | Summary: "Looking to celebrate a holiday in style? Think mini! Grow seedlings in super-small pots for Earth Day. Create cute color bursts for the Hindu festival Holi. Craft cute clay dreidels for Hanukkah. Then use your crafts to mark your favorite festivities. Tiny holiday crafts are tons of fun!"— Provided by publisher.
Identifiers: LCCN 2022051634 (print) | LCCN 2022051635 (ebook) | ISBN 9781669016663 (hardcover) | ISBN 9781669016632 (pdf) | ISBN 9781669016656 (kindle edition) | ISBN 9781669016571 (epub)
Subjects: LCSH: Holiday decorations—Juvenile literature. | Miniature craft—Juvenile literature.
Classification: LCC TT900.H6 F4525 2024 (print) | LCC TT900.H6 (ebook) | DDC 745.5—dc23/eng/20221114
LC record available at https://lccn.loc.gov/2022051634
LC ebook record available at https://lccn.loc.gov/2022051635

Image Credits
iStockphoto: avean (font), Front Cover, 1, Back Cover; Mighty Media, Inc.: project photos; Shutterstock: donatas1205, 5 (right), Feng Yu, 5 (left), TabitaZn, Back Cover (gift tag)

Design Elements
iStockphoto: Tolga TEZCAN; Shutterstock: ds_vector, Valerii_M

Editorial Credits
Editor: Jessica Rusick
Designers: Aruna Rangarajan, Sarah DeYoung

All internet sites appearing in back matter were available and accurate when this book was sent to press.

The publisher and the author shall not be liable for any damages allegedly arising from the information in this book, and they specifically disclaim any liability from the use or application of any of the contents of this book.

TABLE OF CONTENTS

Mini Holidays 4

Mini Color Pouches 6

Mini Earth Day Planters 8

Mini Kinara 10

Mini Carnival Headpiece 12

Mini Pot o' Gold 14

Mini Dreidels 16

Mini New Year's Ball Drop 18

Mini Valentine's Bouquet 20

Mini Ofrenda 24

Mini Chinese New Year Lantern 28

Read More 32

Internet Sites 32

About the Authors 32

MINI HOLIDAYS

Holidays blend traditions, decorations, special foods, and big fun. But what if you could celebrate your favorite holidays on a tiny scale? Infuse even the smallest spaces with holiday joy!

Display a **super-small ofrenda** for Día de los Muertos.

Hang a **teeny lantern** to ring in Chinese New Year.

Or burst **petite pouches of colorful powder** to celebrate Holi.

Whichever holidays you observe, these mini creations will help you **CELEBRATE** in **STYLE!**

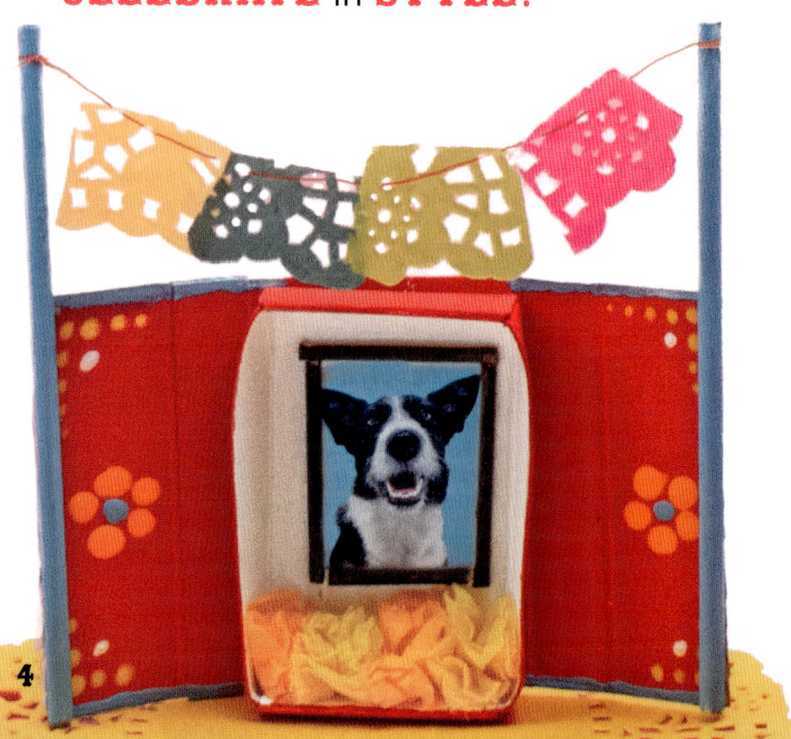

BASIC SUPPLIES

- » beads
- » card stock
- » clay
- » hot glue gun
- » markers
- » paints and paintbrushes
- » ruler
- » scissors
- » string
- » toothpicks

Crafting Tips

SET YOURSELF UP FOR SUCCESS! Read through the materials and instructions before starting a project. Cover your workspace with paper or plastic to protect it from messes or spills.

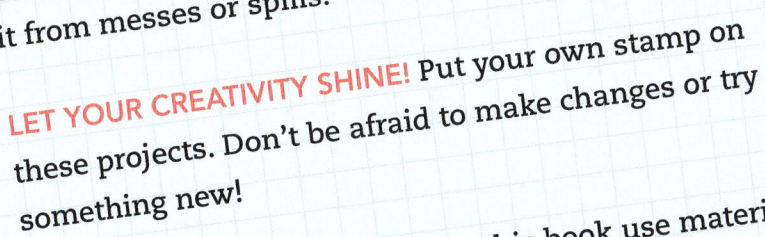

LET YOUR CREATIVITY SHINE! Put your own stamp on these projects. Don't be afraid to make changes or try something new!

UPCYCLE! Lots of the projects in this book use materials you'll likely find around your home. Is there something you can't find? Think of ways to adapt the project using items you do have.

ASK FIRST! Get permission to do the projects and to use any materials you find at home or school.

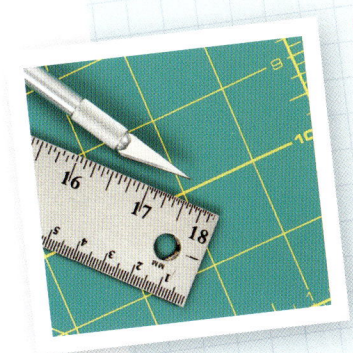

SAFETY FIRST! Ask an adult for help with projects that require sharp or hot tools.

CLEAN UP! When you're finished crafting, make sure to put away any supplies you took out. Clean up any spills and wipe down your crafting surface.

Mini COLOR POUCHES

Holi is a Hindu holiday. It is also called the Festival of Colors. Celebrate Holi by throwing vibrant little powder pouches!

MATERIALS

- » 3 teaspoons (15 milliliters) flour
- » measuring spoon
- » 3 small bowls
- » food dye
- » disposable gloves
- » colorful tissue paper
- » ruler
- » scissors
- » string

1
Pour 1 teaspoon (5 mL) flour into each small bowl.

2
Add a few drops of food dye to each bowl of flour.

3
Wear gloves to mix the dye into each bowl. To make a color more vibrant, add more drops of dye.

4
Allow the mixtures to dry out overnight. Keeping the dried powders separate, use gloved fingers to sift them and break up any chunks.

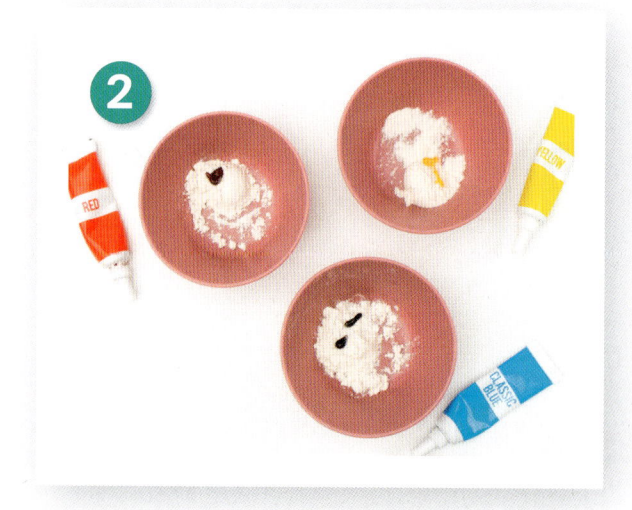

5

For each powder color, cut a 5-by-5-inch (13-by-13-centimeter) square of tissue paper.

6

Cut a 6-inch (15-cm) length of string for each tissue paper square.

7

Pour one colored powder into the center of a tissue paper square. Bring the square's corners up and together and cinch them with one piece of string. Repeat with the other colored powders, tissue paper squares, and pieces of string.

8

Ask an adult for permission to throw your powder pouches against a hard, outdoor surface. Watch as the colors burst!

Mini EARTH DAY PLANTERS

Earth Day is a holiday about protecting the environment. To celebrate, repurpose old paint bottle caps to grow teeny seedlings!

MATERIALS

- » old paint bottles with flip-top, spouted caps
- » paints and paintbrushes
- » soil
- » alfalfa sprout seeds or sunflower seeds
- » small spoon
- » water

1 Clean any paint from inside the caps. It is okay to leave paint on the outsides.

2 Open each cap's top and rest the cap on its bottle. Paint the outside of each cap. Let the paint dry.

3 Remove the caps from the bottles and close each flip top. Use the spoon to fill each cap halfway with soil. Gently press a few seeds into the soil. Then cover the seeds with a thin layer of soil.

4

Open the flip cap on one planter. Hold the cap above the sink. Using the spoon, water the soil, letting any excess water drain from the bottom of the cap into the sink. Close the cap and set the planter in a sunny spot. Repeat with the other planters.

5

Repeat step 4 to water the planters each day.

6

Watch for seedlings to sprout over the next few weeks! When they do, transfer them to larger pots or plant them outside.

TINY TIP

If you don't have old paint bottles, find caps elsewhere! Shampoo bottles often have flip-top, spouted caps.

Mini KINARA

Kwanzaa is a holiday honoring African American culture. Part of the celebration is lighting meaningful candles on a kinara.

MATERIALS
- » air-dry clay
- » ruler
- » stir straws (red, green, black)
- » paint (black or brown) and paintbrush
- » metallic permanent marker (optional)
- » scissors
- » tissue paper (orange, yellow)
- » 4 twist ties

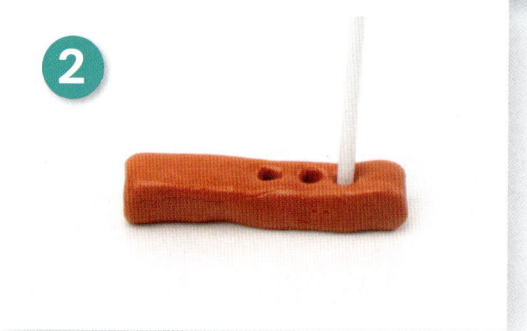

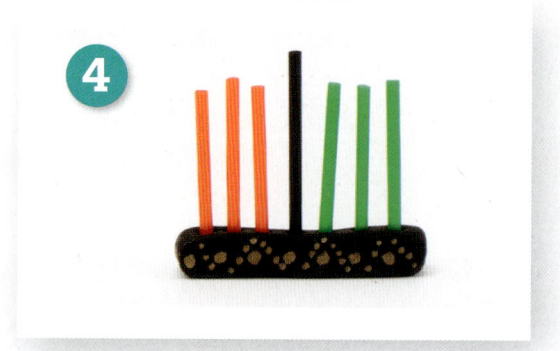

1
Shape air-dry clay into a block that is 2 inches (5 cm) long, ½ inch (1.3 cm) wide, and ¼ inch (0.6 cm) thick. Flatten the block's sides against a hard surface.

2
Use a stir straw to poke seven evenly spaced holes in the top of the block.

3
Let the clay dry overnight. Paint it brown or black. Decorate it with metallic accents if you'd like. This is the kinara's base.

4
Cut three red stir straw pieces and three green stir straw pieces that are 1½ inches (4 cm) long. Cut one slightly longer black stir straw piece. These are the candles. Place the black candle in the kinara's center hole. Place the green candles in the holes on the right. Place the red candles in the holes on the left.

5

Cut 12 to 18 triangles out of orange and yellow tissue paper. Make each side of the triangles about 1 inch (2.5 cm) long.

6

Cut the twist ties in half.

7

Stack two to three triangles on top of each other. Wrap one end of a twist tie piece around the triangles. Leave the rest of the twist tie pointing down. This will fit inside a candle later. Crinkle and trim the paper to make it look like a flame. Repeat this step six times to make seven flames total.

8

You are ready to "light" your kinara! Place a flame's twist tie into a candle opening for each night of Kwanzaa.

Mini CARNIVAL HEADPIECE

MATERIALS
- » craft foam (several colors)
- » pencil
- » ruler
- » scissors
- » craft glue
- » gems
- » glitter
- » feathers
- » string

Carnival is celebrated in many cultures. People often wear colorful, glittering, and feathered costumes at Carnival parades!

1

Draw a headpiece shape on craft foam and cut it out. The shape should be about 1½ inches (3.8 cm) wide.

2

Cut out small shapes in different colors of craft foam. Glue them to the headpiece.

3

Glue gems onto the headpiece.

4

Glue glitter and small feather bits to the headpiece.

5

Cut a length of string twice as long as the headpiece is wide. Glue the ends of the string to the back of the headpiece.

6

Your Carnival headpiece is ready! Tie it onto your finger as a ring. Or use it to dress up one of your toys!

Mini POT O' GOLD

MATERIALS
- » dauber cap
- » 3 small round beads
- » hot glue gun
- » green paint and paintbrush
- » craft glue
- » paper plate
- » gold glitter
- » buttons
- » tweezers
- » parchment paper
- » clear, flexible plastic container lid
- » scissors
- » paint pens (rainbow colors)

Saint Patrick's Day is an Irish holiday. The holiday has a legend that a leprechaun and pot of gold can be found at the end of a rainbow!

1
Hot glue the beads to the bottom of the cap as legs. Make sure the cap can balance on the beads.

2
Paint the cap and beads green.

3
Squeeze glue onto the paper plate. Pour glitter next to the glue. Use tweezers to hold the buttons as you brush them with glue, then dip them in glitter to make gold coins. Set the beads on parchment paper and let the glue dry.

14

4

Cut the clear lid in half. Recycle one half. Cut out a small arch from the other half.

5

Use paint pens to color a rainbow on the arch.

6

Position the rainbow so it stays upright. Fill the pot with the coins. Then place your little pot o' gold at the end of the rainbow!

TINY TIP
Dauber caps can be found on dot markers, bingo markers, bath paint bottles, and bubble bath bottles.

Mini DREIDELS

Hanukkah is a Jewish festival that lasts eight days. Celebrate by making tiny tops to play the holiday's traditional dreidel game!

MATERIALS
- » air-dry clay
- » craft knife
- » mini wooden dowels
- » scissors
- » paint pens (blue, white, gold, silver)

1
Form air-dry clay into a ball about the size of a grape.

2
Use the craft knife to shape one half of the ball. Create four flat, triangular sides that meet in a point.

3
Cut the other half of the ball into a cube shape.

4
Repeat steps 1 through 3 to make as many dreidels as you'd like.

5

Cut the mini dowels in half. Push the cut end of each piece into the flat top of each dreidel.

6

Let the clay dry overnight. Then paint each side of each dreidel in a traditional Hanukkah color: blue, white, silver, and gold. Assign each color to stand for a different dreidel game symbol: nun, gimel, hey, and shin. Paint the handles of the dreidels too. Let the paint dry. You're ready to play!

HOW TO PLAY

Divide 10 to 15 tokens evenly between players. Tokens can be nuts, pennies, or other small items. On their turn, a player puts one token in the center, or pot. Then they spin the dreidel. Nun means the player does nothing. Gimel means the player takes the entire pot. Hey means the player takes half the pot. Shin means the player adds another token to the pot. A player is out when they have no more tokens. **The player who gets all the tokens wins!**

Mini NEW YEAR'S BALL DROP

Midnight on New Year's Eve marks the end of the yearly calendar. Make a sparkling, bitty ball drop to count down to this holiday!

MATERIALS

- » medium round bead
- » mini wooden dowel
- » paints (silver, other colors) and paintbrush
- » sparkly pipe cleaners
- » stapler
- » craft glue
- » paper plate
- » glitter
- » 3 mini clothespins
- » fine-point permanent marker
- » craft foam
- » scissors
- » hot glue gun

1
Paint the bead and dowel silver. Let the paint dry.

2
Wrap one end of four pipe cleaners around the bottom of the dowel.

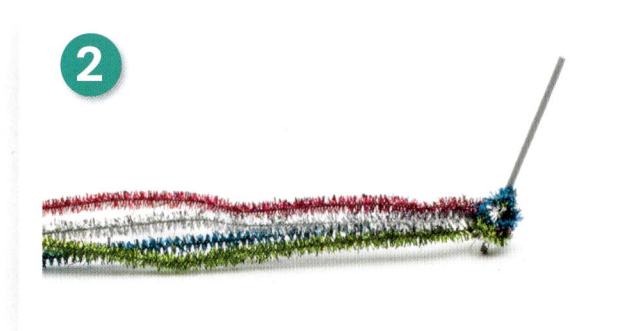

3
Twist the pipe cleaners together and wrap them around the dowel. Make the spiral wider at the bottom of the dowel to create a base. Staple the spiral together.

4
Pour glue onto the paper plate. Pour glitter next to the glue. Brush glue onto the bead. Roll it in the glitter.

5

Paint the mini clothespins and let them dry.

6

Write 1, 2, and 3 on the clothespins.

7

Cut out the letters N, Y, and E from craft foam. These stand for "New Year's Eve." Hot glue the letters to the pipe cleaner spiral.

8

Clip the clothespins to the dowel so they are evenly spaced. Place the "3" clothespin near the top of the dowel, the "2" clothespin in the middle, and the "1" clothespin near the bottom. Then place the glittered bead on top of the dowel.

9

On New Year's Eve, start the countdown at 10 p.m. Remove the "3" clothespin so the ball drops to the "2" clothespin. Remove that clothespin at 11 p.m. Remove the last clothespin when the clock strikes midnight. Happy new year!

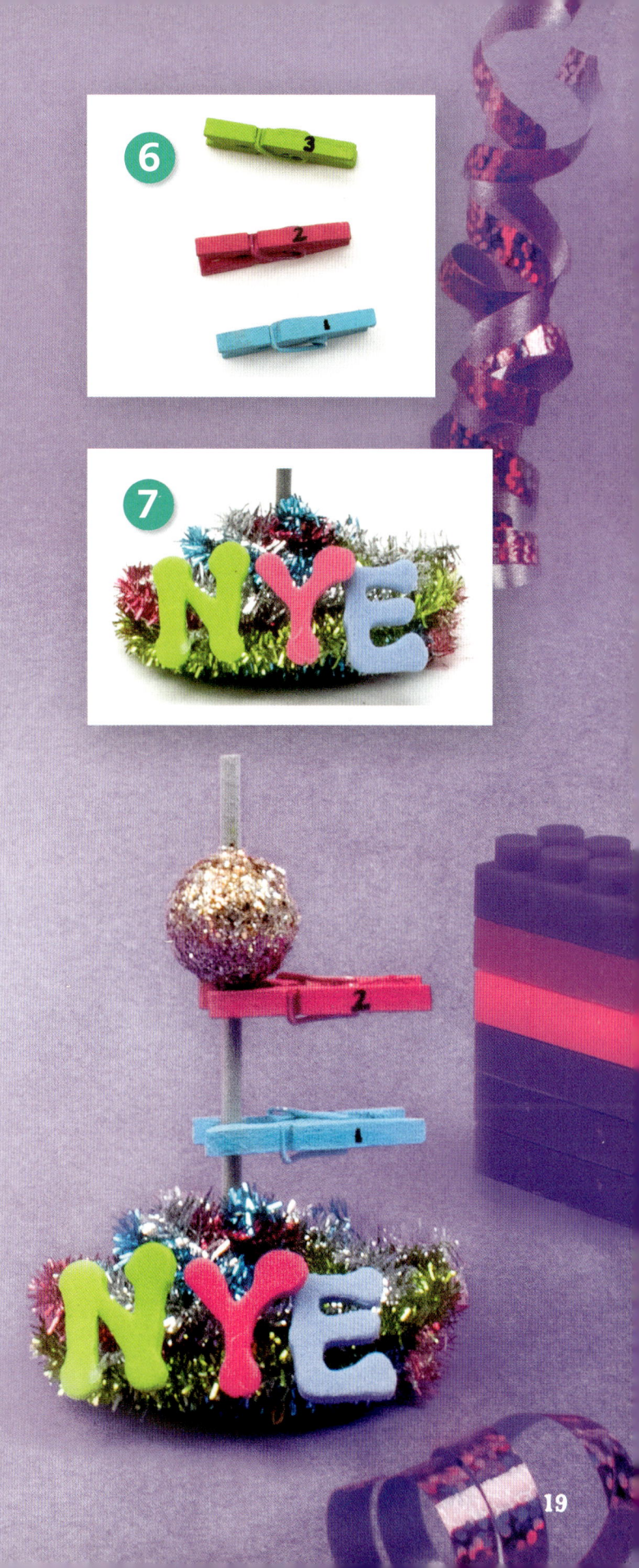

Mini VALENTINE'S BOUQUET

MATERIALS
- » tissue paper (several colors)
- » scissors
- » floral wire
- » washi tape

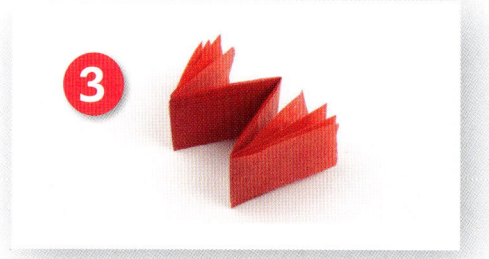

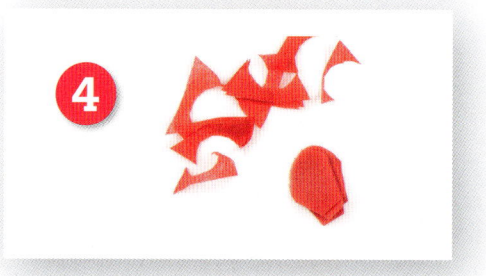

Valentine's Day is a day to celebrate affection. Twist teeny tissue into paper flowers and give someone you love a little bouquet!

1
Cut a square of tissue paper about the size of your palm.

2
Accordion fold the square into a rectangle.

3
Accordion fold the rectangle the opposite way to make a zig-zag shape.

4
Compress the zig-zag shape with the unfolded ends pointing up. Starting at the bottom folded edges, cut the compressed zig-zag shape into a petal shape.

5

Unfold the cutout. You'll have several pairs of petals that are connected in the middle.

6

Stack two petal pieces into an X and twist them together.

7

Repeat step 6 with two additional petal pieces. Then twist together this piece and the one from step 6 to form a flower.

8

Cut a piece of floral wire about as long as your palm. Wrap one end around the flower's center to create a stem.

9

Fluff the petals to cover the wire and add dimension to the flower.

10

Repeat steps 1 through 9 to create more flowers in different colors.

CONTINUED ON THE NEXT PAGE »

11

Bundle the flower stems and wrap a piece of washi tape around them.

12

Wrap up your bouquet! Cut two square pieces of tissue paper about the size of your palm. Stack them slightly off-center from one another in a diamond shape. Fold the bottom point up slightly past the center.

13

Lay the bouquet on top of the tissue paper. The flowers should stick out above the top point. Wrap the sides around the flower stems to make a cone shape. Secure the cone with washi tape.

14

Cut a heart from tissue paper. Tape it to the front of the bouquet wrapping.

15

Your bouquet is ready to be gifted! On Valentine's Day, give it to someone you care about.

TINY TIP
Use unique, decorative tissue paper to give your bouquet wrapping a special pop!

Mini OFRENDA

MATERIALS
- » tissue paper (orange, yellow)
- » ruler
- » scissors
- » matchbox
- » paints and paintbrushes
- » small photo or drawing of a loved one who has passed away
- » toothpicks
- » craft glue
- » hot glue gun
- » colored paper doilies
- » string
- » stir straw

Día de los Muertos is a Mexican holiday. It honors the lives of loved ones who have passed away.

1
Fold the tissue paper so there are several layers. Cut out circles from the tissue paper that are 2 inches (4 cm) wide.

2
Stack two circles on top of each other and pinch the stack's center. Fold and crinkle the paper upward to create a magnolia flower. Repeat to make enough flowers to fill one short end of the matchbox tray. Set the flowers aside.

3
Paint the outside of the matchbox tray. Let it dry.

4
Trim the photo or drawing to fit inside the matchbox tray.

5

Cut the toothpicks into four pieces to frame the photo.

6

Paint the toothpick pieces and let them dry. Then glue the photo inside the matchbox tray. Glue the toothpick pieces around the photo to make a frame. Glue the flowers beneath the frame.

7

Cut the top of the matchbox cover in half.

8

Paint the matchbox cover. Add decorative details to the edges and inner flaps if you'd like.

CONTINUED ON THE NEXT PAGE »

25

9

Hot glue the back of the matchbox tray to the inside center of the matchbox cover.

10

Cut small rectangles from the punched areas of the doilies. These are papel picado flags. *Papel picado* means "punched paper" in Spanish.

11

Thread the papel picado flags onto a piece of string to make a banner.

12

Cut a stir straw in half. Paint the pieces and let them dry.

13

Hot glue the straw pieces along the outer vertical edges of the matchbox cover. The straw's extra length should reach above the matchbox.

26

14

Tie the papel picado banner to the tops of the stir straws.

15

Your mini ofrenda is complete! Display it on Día de los Muertos to honor the loved one it features.

TINY TIP
If you'd like, make more flowers or flags to scatter around the mini ofrenda. You can also add items that remind you of your loved one.

Mini CHINESE NEW YEAR LANTERN

MATERIALS
» red card stock
» pencil
» ruler
» paint pens (black and gold)
» scissors
» mini hole punch
» wire (black or gold)
» gold beads

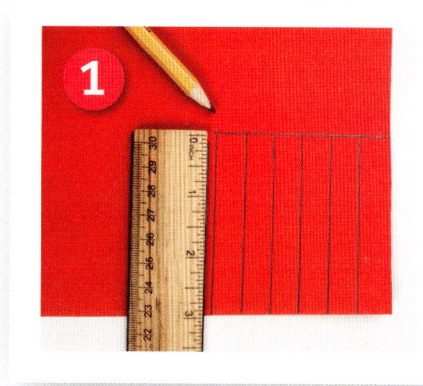

Chinese New Year is a festival ringing in the new year on the Chinese solar calendar. Make a little lantern to hang during this 15-day celebration!

1
Draw six rectangular strips on the card stock. Each should be ½ inch by 3 inches (1.2 by 8 cm).

2
Draw designs on the strips in pencil. Look up Chinese New Year decorations for ideas if you'd like.

3
Trace over the designs in black and gold paint pen.

4

Cut out the strips. Punch a hole in both ends of each strip. Try to place the holes in identical spots.

5

Fold the top ¾ inch (2 cm) and bottom ¾ inch (2 cm) of each strip upward.

6

Thread a piece of wire through one hole in each strip.

7

Thread a bead onto the wire so it sits on top of the strips. Make a loop with the wire and thread it back through the bead from underneath. Pull the wire taut. This will hold the bead in place.

CONTINUED ON THE NEXT PAGE »

8

Thread three or four more beads beneath the strips. Then thread the wire through the bottom holes of the strips.

30

9

Repeat step 7 to add a bead to the bottom of the lantern. Fan out the strips so they are evenly spaced.

10

Trim the wire to the length you'd like and make a loop in the top. Your mini lantern is ready to hang!

TINY TIP
Depending on the size of your beads, you may choose to use more or fewer inside the lantern.

READ MORE

Borgert-Spaniol, Megan. *Winter Crafts Across Cultures: 12 Projects to Celebrate the Season*. North Mankato, MN: Capstone Press, 2023.

DePalma, Kate. *Let's Celebrate!: Special Days Around the World*. Cambridge, MA: Barefoot Books, 2019.

Kukla, Lauren. *Mini Gifts that Surprise and Delight*. North Mankato, MN: Capstone Press, 2023.

INTERNET SITES

Holiday Crafts Archives
achildsworldnc.com/tag/holiday-crafts/

Holidays for Kids: List of Days
www.ducksters.com/holidays/kids_calendar.php

Special Days and Holidays
funfamilycrafts.com/special-days-and-holidays/

ABOUT THE AUTHORS

Rebecca Felix is an author and editor of children's books. She loves brainstorming crafts, taking hikes, camping, and learning about all kinds of topics! She collects houseplants in her Minnesota home, where she lives with her funny husband, joyful daughter, and sleepy dog.

Ruthie Van Oosbree is a writer and editor who loves making crafts. In her free time, she enjoys doing word puzzles, reading, and playing the piano. She lives with her husband and three cats in the Twin Cities.